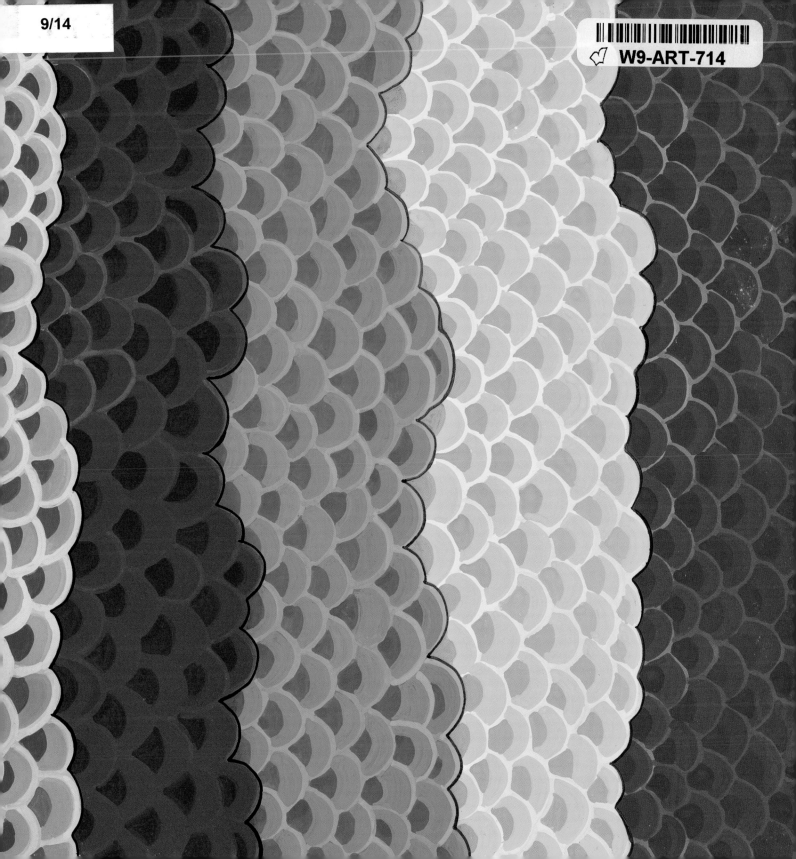

For Foong Sze, Foong Yann, Sheng Zhou and all children
who delight in the colors around them. —R. T.

To Linda S. Wingerter, who, when I asked her to pick a color,
always chose green. —G. L.

Amicus Illustrated is published by Amicus
P.O. Box 1329 Mankato, MN 56002
www.amicuspublishing.us

This library-bound edition is reprinted by arrangement with Chronicle Books LLC, 680 Second Street, San Francisco, California 94107.

First published in the United States in 2001 by Chronicle Books LLC.

Book design by Sara Gillingham.
Typeset in Albertus.
The illustrations in this book were rendered in gouache.

Library of Congress Cataloging-in-Publication Data
Thong, Roseanne.
Red is a dragon : a book of colors / by Roseanne Thong ; illustrated by Grace Lin.
pages cm. -- (Multicultural shapes and colors)
Originally published in 2001 by Chronicle Books.
Summary: A Chinese American girl provides rhyming descriptions of the great variety of colors she sees around her,
from the red of a dragon, firecrackers, and lychees to the brown of her teddy bear.
ISBN 978-1-60753-565-2 (library binding)
[1. Stories in rhyme. 2. Color--Fiction. 3. Chinese Americans--Fiction.] I. Lin, Grace, illustrator. II. Title.
PZ8.3.T328Re 2014
[E]--dc23
2014001004

Printed in the United States of America at
Corporate Graphics, North Mankato, Minnesota.
10 9 8 7 6 5 4 3 2 1

Red Is a Dragon

A Book of Colors

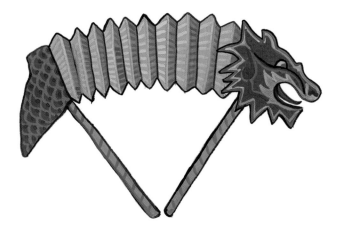

written by Roseanne Thong illustrated by Grace Lin

Red is a dragon
Red is a drum
Red are the firecrackers—
here they come!

Red are melons
cool and sweet
Red are lychees
a summer treat

Orange are the crabs
    that dance in the sand
And so is the seashell
    I hold in my hand

Yellow are incense sticks
and flowers
Yellow are flames
that burn for hours

Yellow are raincoats
and bright rubber boots
Yellow is a taxi
that honks and toots

Green are the toads
beneath my pail
Bottle gourds
and crunchy kale

Green is a bracelet
made of jade
Green is the purse
my auntie made

Blue is a pool
    for making a wish
Dragonflies and
    shimmering fish

Blue are the sneakers
on my shelf
Blue is the ribbon
I won myself

Purple are clouds
  at the end of the day
Purple is a kite
  that sails away

Pink is a peony
Pink is a rose
Pink is the sunlight
on my nose

Pink are an opera
singer's eyes
And a silk fan
that hides her surprise

Brown is my grandpa's
hat I wear
Brown is my favorite
teddy bear

White are noodles
and chopsticks, too
White are dumplings
for me and you!

The world is a rainbow
for us to explore
What colors are waiting
outside your door?

SOME OF THE WORDS FOUND IN THIS BOOK

Bottle gourd: A pear-shaped vegetable eaten in soups, stir-fried or boiled. It is often pictured in Chinese design and art.

Chopsticks: Two thin sticks used to pick up food. They are usually made of wood, plastic or bamboo.

Dragon: Chinese dragons help people rather than harm them. A New Year dragon dance brings good luck and scares away evil spirits.

Dumplings: Small pockets of dough filled with meat or vegetables, shaped like half moons.

Firecrackers: Chinese firecrackers are tiny red cylinders that hang in long strings. Their loud cracking noise is thought to chase away bad luck.

Incense sticks: Sandalwood sticks that give off a sweet-smelling smoke when burned. They are used for prayer or worship.

Jade: A hard, usually green- or white-colored gemstone used to make jewelry and art objects. It is thought to offer protection to those who keep it.

Lychee: A small, oval fruit from Southern China that grows on trees and ripens in early summer. It has bumpy red skin and a sweet white translucent center.

Peony: Known as the "queen of flowers," the peony is a popular Chinese flower. It represents springtime and wealth.

Silk fans: Fans have been used in China for more than three thousand years. After the invention of silk, artists and scholars began to decorate silk fans with poetry and pictures.

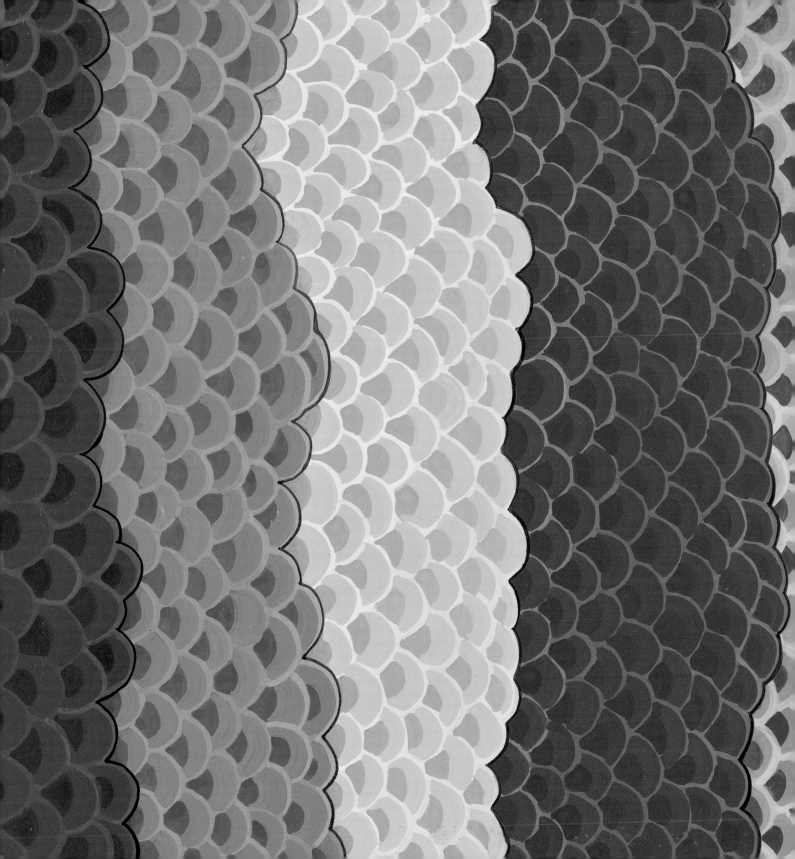